North American A...

Billy Grinslott & Kinsey Marie Books
ISBN 9781957881478

There are many squirrels in the wild. The most popular is the gray squirrel. Squirrels are very acrobatic and can climb trees. Their favorite food is acorns.

Chipmunks are small members of the squirrel family. They have pouches inside of their cheeks so they can carry food. They are very friendly and will take food from your hand.

This is a Gopher. Gophers are little excavators. They have sharp claws and make tunnels and burrows underground. That's where they live most of the time.

Prairie dogs live in tight-knit family groups called coteries. Their vocabulary is more advanced than any other animal language. They got their name because they live on the prairies and their warning calls which sound like dog barks. They build mounds around their den to keep water out.

Groundhogs are the largest member of the squirrel family. Groundhogs get their name because of their big bodies, and they live underground. Groundhog Day is where Punxsutawney Phil predicts how long winter will last.

Badgers live underground with other family members. Badgers are very social and live in groups. A badger den or sett can be centuries old and are used by many generations of badgers.

Pee-ewe what is that stinky critter with the big bushy tail. It smells bad. Skunks are normally curious and friendly unless you scare them. If you scare them, they will flip their bushy tale at you and spray you with a smelly potion and it stinks.

Porcupines have sharp quills on their backs to help protect them. A porcupine can have up to 30 thousand quills, they are sharp and will stick you if you touch them. To communicate they make grunts and high-pitched noises. A group of porcupines is called a family.

Opossums or possums have strong tails and can hang from trees. One trick that a possum has, is when it feels danger is it will play dead. It will lay there and not move. Possums have white to gray face hair. Possums like to eat wood ticks. They are also immune to snakebites.

Hey what is that with the mask around its eyes. That is a raccoon. Raccoons like to come out at night. Their eyes are made so they can see in the dark. They are called masked bandits because they like to raid and eat out of trash cans at night.

There are many types of rabbits in the wild. The most common is the cottontail. Rabbits are cute, friendly, and fun to watch. Many people have rabbits for pets. They have soft fluffy fur.

The hare is a bigger rabbit with longer ears and legs. Their longs legs help them to run fast. They are agile and faster than most rabbits.

Armadillos get their name because their shell is like wearing armor. When they feel endangered, they roll up into a ball and their hard shell protects them. Armadillos hate the cold and live in warm areas. They sleep up to 16 hours a day.

Beavers use their teeth to cut and knock down trees. They build dams with them to block water, so they have a place to live and swim. They also eat wood. Beavers can stay underwater for about 8 minutes. Beavers slap their tails on the water to indicate danger. Beavers are the largest rodents in North America.

A wolverine's color patterns are unique. No wolverine has the same fur color as another. Wolverines don't hibernate in the winter. They sleep in caves, rock crevices, or under fallen trees. Wolverines have a keen sense of smell that can detect another animal 20 feet under the snow. Wolverines have poor eyesight and are active at night. Wolverine babies are called kits. They are born with white fur that turns brown as they age.

Bobcats are frequently misidentified as a lynx. Bobcats are part of the lynx family, but they are smaller than a lynx with different markings.

The Lynx is larger than its relative the bobcat and has lighter fur and more spots than a bobcat.

The mountain lion, also known as the cougar is one of the biggest cats in North America. Mountain lions don't roar like other big cats they communicate in different ways, such as chirping, growling, shrieking, and even purring.

There are several types of foxes in North America. This is a red fox. Females are called vixens. Red foxes have supersonic hearing. When afraid, red foxes grin or look like they are smiling. Red foxes front paws have five toes, while their hind feet only have four.

The coyote is bigger than a fox. Eastern coyotes are part wolf. Coyotes are great for pest control, they like to eat mice and rats. They can adapt and live almost anywhere, even in the city.

Wolves, coyotes, and foxes are all part of the dog family. The timber wolf, also known as the gray wolf, is the largest wolf in North America. Wolves are legendary because of their spine-tingling howl, which they use to communicate. Their territory size is 25 to 150 square miles. They like to roam in packs of 2 to 25 wolves.

There are several types of antelopes, this one is known as the pronghorn. Antelopes have extremely developed senses which help them detect danger. They are quick runners and can run up to 45 mph. They all like to live in herds. Antelopes don't outrun other animals, they out maneuver them. They can twist and turn very quickly. They are related to cows, sheep, and goats.

The bighorn sheep is part of the sheep family and likes to live in mountainous areas. Females are called ewes and males are called rams. They are called rams because they like to use their horns to slam into things. Their horn size is a symbol of how high they rank in the herd. The bigger their horns are, the higher they rank.

The whitetail deer is the most popular deer in North America. Whitetail deer have good eyesight and hearing. Only male deer grow antlers, which are shed each year. Whitetail deer are good swimmers and will use large streams and lakes to escape predators. A young deer is called a fawn. They are the most common deer species and live everywhere in North America.

Mule deer get their name because of their mule like ears. Male deer are called bucks and females are does. Males grow new antlers every year. They can run 30 miles per hour. They are bigger than whitetail deer and prefer living in the mountain areas.

Weighing in at up to 700 pounds, the North American Elk is one of the biggest deer species on earth. They can run as fast as 40 miles per hour. They can outrun horses. They make a cool bugling sound when communicating with other elk. It's fun to listen to them.

Moose are huge and weigh up to 800 pounds. Moose love water and are good swimmers. Moose only live in places that have snow cover in the winter. At 5 days old they can outrun a person.

The North American Bison and Buffalo are sometimes confused as the same animal, but they are not. Bison have long hair on their backs, front, and a long beard. Bison are bigger than buffalo. They are the largest mammal in North America and weigh up to 2,000 pounds.

Wild boars are part of the pig family. Wild boars have tusks on their lower and upper lips. The wild boar has long, rubbery snout that is used for digging for food. Wild boars are nocturnal animals, they come out at night. They are very family orientated and like to live in groups called sounds. They have a double coat of fur to help protect them.

Black bears are the smallest members of the bear family in North America. Black Bears love to eat sweet things like berries, fruits, and vegetables. They are good climbers and fast runners. They usually sleep for long periods of time and hibernate during the winter.

Brown bears are often called Grizzley bears, but they're not. Brown bears can grow to seven feet tall. Brown bears eat mostly grass, roots, and berries but will eat fish and other small mammals. They are commonly silent but can communicate with grunts, roars, or squeals.

Grizzley bears are a subspecies of the brown bear. They are called Grizzley bears because they have silver tips on their hair, a grizzled look. The hump on a grizzly bear's back is a huge muscle. Grizzley bears don't hibernate like other bears. They are highly intelligent, have excellent memories and great smell. They are good swimmers and fast runners.

The Polar Bear is the biggest bear on earth. Male polar bears can weigh up to 1500 lbs. Female polar bears weigh about half as much as males. They like swimming and can swim constantly for days at a time. Polar bears keep warm thanks to the blubber under their skin. They can smell up to a mile away. Polar bears spend most of their time at sea. They can run 25 mph and swim up to 10mph. Thanks.

Author Page

North American Animals

Billy Grinslott & Kinsey Marie Books.
Copyright, All Rights Reserved.
ISBN 9781957881478
To Check Out More Our Kids Books.
Visit Kinsey Marie Books or Billy Grinslott.